50 Layered Cakes Made With Love

By: Kelly Johnson

Table of Contents

- Classic Red Velvet Cake
- Chocolate Fudge Layer Cake
- Lemon Blueberry Pound Cake
- Carrot Cake with Cream Cheese Frosting
- Strawberry Shortcake Layer Cake
- Vanilla Bean and Raspberry Jam Cake
- Mocha Coffee Cake
- Funfetti Birthday Cake
- Coconut Cream Layer Cake
- Pineapple Upside-Down Cake
- Apple Cinnamon Spice Cake
- Almond Joy Layer Cake
- Matcha Green Tea Cake
- Salted Caramel Chocolate Cake
- Blueberry Lemon Cake
- Black Forest Cake
- German Chocolate Cake

- Peanut Butter Cup Cake
- Churro Layer Cake
- Hazelnut Praline Cake
- Tiramisu Cake
- Mango Coconut Cake
- Pumpkin Spice Layer Cake
- Raspberry Chocolate Cake
- Orange Creamsicle Layer Cake
- Pina Colada Cake
- Key Lime Cake
- Bourbon Pecan Cake
- Cherry Almond Cake
- Snickers Layer Cake
- White Chocolate Strawberry Cake
- Cookies and Cream Cake
- Zucchini Chocolate Cake
- Coconut Pineapple Cake
- Maple Walnut Cake
- Mocha Hazelnut Cake

- S'mores Layer Cake
- Lavender Honey Cake
- Chocolate Mint Layer Cake
- Lemon Poppy Seed Cake
- Red Wine Chocolate Cake
- Chai Spice Layer Cake
- Lemon Raspberry Cheesecake Cake
- Coffee Hazelnut Cake
- Nutella Hazelnut Cake
- Choco-Mocha Torte
- Mixed Berry Yogurt Cake
- Sweet Potato Spice Cake
- Oreo Cookie Layer Cake
- Cinnamon Roll Layer Cake

Classic Red Velvet Cake

A moist, soft red cake with a rich cream cheese frosting for a perfect balance of sweetness and tang.

Ingredients:

- 2 1/2 cups all-purpose flour
- 1 1/2 cups granulated sugar
- 1 tsp baking soda
- 1 tsp cocoa powder
- 1 1/2 cups vegetable oil
- 1 cup buttermilk, room temperature
- 2 large eggs, room temperature
- 2 tbsp red food coloring
- 1 tsp white vinegar
- 1 tsp vanilla extract
- 1/2 tsp salt

Frosting:

- 8 oz cream cheese, softened
- 1/2 cup unsalted butter, softened
- 4 cups powdered sugar
- 1 tsp vanilla extract

Instructions:

1. Preheat oven to 350°F (175°C). Grease and flour two 9-inch round cake pans.

2. In a large bowl, whisk together the flour, sugar, baking soda, cocoa powder, and salt.

3. In a separate bowl, mix the oil, buttermilk, eggs, food coloring, vinegar, and vanilla extract.

4. Add the wet ingredients to the dry ingredients and mix until just combined.

5. Divide the batter evenly between the two pans and bake for 30-35 minutes or until a toothpick comes out clean.

6. Let the cakes cool in the pans for 10 minutes, then turn them out onto a wire rack to cool completely.

7. For the frosting, beat the cream cheese and butter until smooth. Gradually add powdered sugar and vanilla extract, and beat until fluffy.

8. Frost the cooled cakes and serve.

Chocolate Fudge Layer Cake

A rich and decadent chocolate cake with layers of creamy fudge frosting.

Ingredients:

- 2 cups all-purpose flour
- 1 3/4 cups granulated sugar
- 3/4 cup cocoa powder
- 1 tsp baking powder
- 1 1/2 tsp baking soda
- 1 tsp salt
- 1 cup buttermilk, room temperature
- 1/2 cup vegetable oil
- 2 large eggs
- 1 tsp vanilla extract
- 1 cup hot water

Frosting:

- 1 1/2 cups heavy cream
- 2 cups semi-sweet chocolate chips
- 2 tbsp unsalted butter

Instructions:

1. Preheat oven to 350°F (175°C). Grease and flour two 9-inch round cake pans.

2. In a large bowl, whisk together the flour, sugar, cocoa powder, baking powder, baking soda, and salt.

3. Add the buttermilk, vegetable oil, eggs, and vanilla extract to the dry ingredients, mixing until smooth.

4. Gradually add the hot water, mixing until the batter is thin.

5. Pour the batter evenly into the pans and bake for 30-35 minutes or until a toothpick comes out clean.

6. For the frosting, heat the heavy cream in a saucepan over medium heat until it starts to simmer.

7. Remove from heat and stir in the chocolate chips and butter until smooth.

8. Let the cakes cool, then frost with the chocolate fudge frosting.

Lemon Blueberry Pound Cake

A moist pound cake with fresh blueberries and a burst of lemon flavor.

Ingredients:

- 2 cups all-purpose flour
- 1 tsp baking powder
- 1/2 tsp salt
- 1 cup unsalted butter, softened
- 2 cups granulated sugar
- 4 large eggs, room temperature
- 1 tsp vanilla extract
- 1 tbsp lemon zest
- 1/2 cup sour cream
- 1 cup fresh blueberries

Instructions:

1. Preheat oven to 350°F (175°C). Grease and flour a 9x5-inch loaf pan.
2. In a bowl, whisk together the flour, baking powder, and salt.
3. In a large bowl, cream together the butter and sugar until light and fluffy.
4. Add the eggs one at a time, mixing well after each addition. Stir in the vanilla and lemon zest.
5. Alternate adding the dry ingredients and sour cream, mixing until just combined.

6. Gently fold in the blueberries.

7. Pour the batter into the prepared pan and bake for 60-70 minutes or until a toothpick comes out clean.

8. Let the cake cool before serving.

Carrot Cake with Cream Cheese Frosting

A moist, spiced carrot cake with a tangy cream cheese frosting.

Ingredients:

- 2 cups all-purpose flour
- 1 1/2 tsp baking powder
- 1 1/2 tsp baking soda
- 1 tsp ground cinnamon
- 1/2 tsp ground nutmeg
- 1/2 tsp salt
- 1 1/2 cups granulated sugar
- 1 cup vegetable oil
- 4 large eggs
- 2 cups finely grated carrots
- 1/2 cup chopped walnuts (optional)

Frosting:

- 8 oz cream cheese, softened
- 1/2 cup unsalted butter, softened
- 4 cups powdered sugar
- 1 tsp vanilla extract

Instructions:

1. Preheat oven to 350°F (175°C). Grease and flour two 9-inch round cake pans.

2. In a bowl, whisk together the flour, baking powder, baking soda, cinnamon, nutmeg, and salt.

3. In a separate bowl, mix together the sugar, oil, and eggs until well combined.

4. Stir in the grated carrots and walnuts (if using).

5. Add the dry ingredients to the wet ingredients and mix until just combined.

6. Pour the batter into the pans and bake for 30-35 minutes or until a toothpick comes out clean.

7. For the frosting, beat the cream cheese and butter until smooth. Gradually add powdered sugar and vanilla extract, and beat until fluffy.

8. Frost the cooled cakes and serve.

Strawberry Shortcake Layer Cake

A light and fluffy cake with layers of sweet strawberries and whipped cream.

Ingredients:

- 2 cups all-purpose flour
- 1 1/2 tsp baking powder
- 1/2 tsp salt
- 1 cup unsalted butter, softened
- 1 cup granulated sugar
- 4 large eggs
- 1 tsp vanilla extract
- 1/2 cup milk
- 2 cups fresh strawberries, sliced
- 1/4 cup granulated sugar (for the strawberries)
- 2 cups heavy cream
- 1/4 cup powdered sugar

Instructions:

1. Preheat oven to 350°F (175°C). Grease and flour two 9-inch round cake pans.
2. In a bowl, whisk together the flour, baking powder, and salt.
3. In a separate bowl, cream together the butter and sugar until light and fluffy.

4. Add the eggs one at a time, mixing well after each addition. Stir in the vanilla extract.

5. Alternate adding the dry ingredients and milk, mixing until just combined.

6. Pour the batter into the pans and bake for 30-35 minutes or until a toothpick comes out clean.

7. For the whipped cream, beat the heavy cream and powdered sugar until stiff peaks form.

8. Toss the sliced strawberries with the sugar and let sit for 10 minutes.

9. Once the cakes have cooled, assemble by layering the cake, whipped cream, and strawberries. Top with more whipped cream and strawberries.

Strawberry Shortcake Layer Cake

Ingredients:

- 2 1/2 cups all-purpose flour
- 1 tbsp baking powder
- 1/2 tsp salt
- 1 cup unsalted butter (softened)
- 1 3/4 cups sugar
- 4 eggs
- 1 tbsp vanilla extract
- 1 cup whole milk

Filling & Topping:

- 2 cups heavy cream
- 1/4 cup powdered sugar
- 1 tsp vanilla
- 2 cups fresh strawberries (sliced)

Instructions:

1. Preheat oven to 350°F (175°C). Grease and line two 9-inch pans.
2. Cream butter and sugar. Add eggs one at a time, then vanilla.
3. Alternate adding flour mixture and milk. Pour into pans.

4. Bake 30–35 mins. Cool completely.

5. Whip cream with powdered sugar and vanilla until stiff.

6. Layer with whipped cream and strawberries. Top with more cream and berries.

Vanilla Bean and Raspberry Jam Cake

Ingredients:

- 2 1/2 cups all-purpose flour
- 2 tsp baking powder
- 1/2 tsp salt
- 3/4 cup butter
- 1 1/2 cups sugar
- 4 eggs
- 1 tbsp vanilla bean paste
- 1 cup milk

Filling & Frosting:

- 3/4 cup raspberry jam
- 1/2 cup butter
- 8 oz cream cheese
- 1 tsp vanilla
- 3 cups powdered sugar

Instructions:

1. Preheat to 350°F (175°C). Line two 8-inch cake pans.

2. Make batter as usual: cream butter and sugar, add eggs, vanilla bean, milk, and dry ingredients.

3. Bake 30–35 minutes. Cool.

4. Spread jam between layers, then frost with cream cheese frosting.

Mocha Coffee Cake

Ingredients:

- 2 cups all-purpose flour
- 1/2 cup cocoa powder
- 2 tsp baking powder
- 1/2 tsp baking soda
- 1/2 tsp salt
- 3/4 cup butter
- 1 1/4 cups sugar
- 3 eggs
- 1 tsp vanilla
- 3/4 cup brewed coffee (cooled)
- 1/2 cup sour cream

Frosting:

- 1/2 cup butter
- 1/4 cup cocoa
- 2 tbsp coffee
- 2 1/2 cups powdered sugar

Instructions:

1. Preheat oven to 350°F (175°C). Prepare two 8-inch pans.

2. Combine dry ingredients. Cream butter and sugar, add eggs, vanilla, coffee, and sour cream.

3. Pour into pans and bake 30 minutes. Cool. Frost with mocha icing.

Funfetti Birthday Cake

Ingredients:

- 2 1/2 cups all-purpose flour
- 1 tbsp baking powder
- 1/2 tsp salt
- 1 cup butter
- 1 3/4 cups sugar
- 4 egg whites
- 1 tbsp vanilla
- 1 cup milk
- 3/4 cup rainbow sprinkles

Frosting:

- 1 cup butter
- 3 1/2 cups powdered sugar
- 1 tbsp milk
- 1 tsp vanilla
- Extra sprinkles for topping

Instructions:

1. Preheat oven to 350°F (175°C). Line three 8-inch pans.

2. Cream butter and sugar. Add egg whites, vanilla, milk. Stir in dry ingredients, fold in sprinkles.

3. Bake 25–30 mins. Cool. Frost and top with more sprinkles.

Coconut Cream Layer Cake

Ingredients:

- 2 1/2 cups cake flour
- 2 tsp baking powder
- 1/2 tsp salt
- 1/2 cup butter
- 1/2 cup coconut oil
- 1 3/4 cups sugar
- 4 eggs
- 1 tsp coconut extract
- 1 cup coconut milk
- 1 cup shredded coconut

Frosting:

- 8 oz cream cheese
- 1/2 cup butter
- 1 tsp vanilla
- 1 tsp coconut extract
- 3 cups powdered sugar
- 1 cup toasted coconut (for garnish)

Instructions:

1. Preheat to 350°F (175°C). Grease two 9-inch pans.

2. Cream butter, oil, and sugar. Add eggs, coconut extract. Alternate coconut milk and dry mix.

3. Fold in shredded coconut. Bake 30–35 mins. Cool.

4. Frost and top with toasted coconut.

Pineapple Upside-Down Cake

A sweet, caramelized pineapple topping on a moist, buttery cake.

Ingredients:

- 1/4 cup unsalted butter
- 1 cup brown sugar
- 1 can (20 oz) pineapple rings, drained (reserve juice)
- Maraschino cherries (optional, for garnish)
- 1 1/2 cups all-purpose flour
- 1 tsp baking powder
- 1/2 tsp salt
- 1/2 cup unsalted butter, softened
- 1 cup granulated sugar
- 2 large eggs
- 1 tsp vanilla extract
- 1/2 cup reserved pineapple juice
- 1/2 cup whole milk

Instructions:

1. Preheat oven to 350°F (175°C). Grease and flour a 9-inch round cake pan.
2. In a small saucepan, melt 1/4 cup butter over medium heat. Stir in brown sugar until it begins to bubble. Pour this mixture into the prepared cake pan.

3. Arrange the pineapple rings over the sugar mixture, placing a cherry in the center of each ring.

4. In a bowl, whisk together the flour, baking powder, and salt.

5. In a separate bowl, cream the softened butter and granulated sugar until light and fluffy. Add the eggs one at a time, mixing well after each addition, followed by vanilla extract.

6. Alternate adding the dry ingredients and milk, starting and ending with the dry ingredients. Mix until just combined.

7. Pour the batter over the pineapple rings and smooth the top.

8. Bake for 35-40 minutes or until a toothpick inserted comes out clean.

9. Let cool for 10 minutes before inverting the cake onto a plate.

Apple Cinnamon Spice Cake

A warm, spiced apple cake with a hint of cinnamon and nutmeg.

Ingredients:

- 1 1/2 cups all-purpose flour
- 1 tsp baking powder
- 1 tsp ground cinnamon
- 1/2 tsp ground nutmeg
- 1/4 tsp salt
- 1/2 cup unsalted butter, softened
- 1 cup granulated sugar
- 2 large eggs
- 1 tsp vanilla extract
- 1/2 cup applesauce
- 1 1/2 cups diced apples (peeled)

Instructions:

1. Preheat oven to 350°F (175°C). Grease and flour a 9-inch round cake pan.
2. In a bowl, whisk together the flour, baking powder, cinnamon, nutmeg, and salt.
3. In a separate bowl, cream the butter and sugar until light and fluffy. Add the eggs, one at a time, mixing well after each addition, followed by vanilla extract.

4. Gradually add the dry ingredients to the wet mixture, alternating with the applesauce. Fold in the diced apples.

5. Pour the batter into the prepared pan and bake for 30-35 minutes, or until a toothpick comes out clean.

6. Allow the cake to cool before serving.

Almond Joy Layer Cake

A decadent cake with chocolate, coconut, and almond layers, inspired by the classic candy bar.

Ingredients:

- 2 cups all-purpose flour
- 1 1/2 cups granulated sugar
- 1 tsp baking powder
- 1/2 tsp baking soda
- 1/2 tsp salt
- 1/2 cup unsweetened cocoa powder
- 1/2 cup vegetable oil
- 2 large eggs
- 1 tsp vanilla extract
- 1 cup buttermilk
- 1/2 cup boiling water
- 1 cup shredded coconut
- 1/2 cup chopped almonds

Frosting:

- 2 cups semi-sweet chocolate chips
- 1/2 cup heavy cream

- 1/4 cup unsalted butter

Instructions:

1. Preheat oven to 350°F (175°C). Grease and flour two 9-inch round cake pans.

2. In a large bowl, whisk together the flour, sugar, baking powder, baking soda, salt, and cocoa powder.

3. Add the oil, eggs, vanilla extract, and buttermilk, and mix until smooth. Gradually add the boiling water and stir to combine.

4. Fold in the shredded coconut and chopped almonds.

5. Divide the batter evenly between the two pans and bake for 30-35 minutes or until a toothpick comes out clean.

6. For the frosting, heat the chocolate chips, heavy cream, and butter in a saucepan over medium heat, stirring until melted and smooth.

7. Let the cakes cool before frosting with the chocolate mixture.

Matcha Green Tea Cake

A vibrant green cake infused with earthy matcha flavor.

Ingredients:

- 2 cups all-purpose flour
- 1 1/2 tsp baking powder
- 1/4 tsp salt
- 2 tbsp matcha powder
- 1 cup unsalted butter, softened
- 1 cup granulated sugar
- 3 large eggs
- 1 tsp vanilla extract
- 1/2 cup whole milk
- 1/2 cup sour cream

Frosting:

- 8 oz cream cheese, softened
- 1/2 cup unsalted butter, softened
- 3 cups powdered sugar
- 1-2 tbsp matcha powder (optional, for flavor)

Instructions:

1. Preheat oven to 350°F (175°C). Grease and flour two 9-inch round cake pans.

2. In a bowl, whisk together the flour, baking powder, salt, and matcha powder.

3. In a separate bowl, cream the butter and sugar until light and fluffy. Add the eggs one at a time, mixing well after each addition, followed by vanilla extract.

4. Alternate adding the dry ingredients and milk, starting and ending with the dry ingredients. Mix until just combined.

5. Fold in the sour cream until smooth.

6. Divide the batter between the pans and bake for 25-30 minutes, or until a toothpick comes out clean.

7. For the frosting, beat the cream cheese and butter until smooth, then gradually add powdered sugar and matcha powder until well combined.

8. Frost the cooled cakes and serve.

Salted Caramel Chocolate Cake

A rich chocolate cake with layers of smooth salted caramel frosting.

Ingredients:

- 2 cups all-purpose flour
- 1 1/2 tsp baking powder
- 1 tsp baking soda
- 1/2 tsp salt
- 1 cup unsweetened cocoa powder
- 1 cup granulated sugar
- 1/2 cup unsalted butter, softened
- 2 large eggs
- 1 tsp vanilla extract
- 1 cup buttermilk
- 1 cup hot water

Frosting:

- 1/2 cup unsalted butter
- 1 cup brown sugar
- 1/2 cup heavy cream
- 1 tsp vanilla extract

- 1/4 tsp sea salt

- 3 cups powdered sugar

Instructions:

1. Preheat oven to 350°F (175°C). Grease and flour two 9-inch round cake pans.

2. In a bowl, whisk together the flour, baking powder, baking soda, salt, cocoa powder, and sugar.

3. In a separate bowl, mix the butter, eggs, and vanilla extract until smooth. Add the buttermilk and mix.

4. Gradually add the dry ingredients to the wet ingredients, alternating with the hot water. Mix until just combined.

5. Pour the batter evenly between the pans and bake for 30-35 minutes or until a toothpick comes out clean.

6. For the frosting, melt the butter and brown sugar in a saucepan over medium heat. Stir in the heavy cream and vanilla extract, then bring to a simmer. Simmer for 5-7 minutes, then remove from heat.

7. Stir in the sea salt, then gradually add powdered sugar until smooth.

8. Frost the cooled cakes with salted caramel frosting.

Blueberry Lemon Cake

Ingredients:

- 2 ½ cups all-purpose flour
- 2 tsp baking powder
- ½ tsp baking soda
- ½ tsp salt
- ¾ cup unsalted butter (softened)
- 1 ½ cups granulated sugar
- 3 eggs
- 1 tsp vanilla extract
- 1 tbsp lemon zest
- 2 tbsp lemon juice
- 1 cup buttermilk
- 1 ½ cups fresh or frozen blueberries (tossed with 1 tbsp flour)

Lemon Cream Cheese Frosting:

- 8 oz cream cheese
- ½ cup unsalted butter
- 1 tsp vanilla
- 1 tbsp lemon juice

- 3–4 cups powdered sugar

Instructions:

1. Preheat oven to 350°F (175°C). Grease and flour two 8-inch pans.
2. Cream butter and sugar, then beat in eggs, vanilla, lemon zest, and juice.
3. Alternate adding flour mixture and buttermilk until smooth.
4. Fold in blueberries. Divide batter between pans.
5. Bake 30–35 minutes or until a toothpick comes out clean.
6. Cool completely and frost with lemon cream cheese frosting.

Black Forest Cake

Ingredients:

- 1 ¾ cups all-purpose flour
- ¾ cup cocoa powder
- 2 tsp baking soda
- 1 tsp baking powder
- ½ tsp salt
- ¾ cup buttermilk
- ½ cup vegetable oil
- 2 eggs
- 2 tsp vanilla extract
- 1 cup hot coffee
- 1 ½ cups sugar

Filling & Topping:

- 2 cups heavy whipping cream
- ¼ cup powdered sugar
- 1 tsp vanilla
- 1 ½ cups cherry pie filling or sweet dark cherries
- Chocolate shavings and extra cherries for garnish

Instructions:

1. Preheat oven to 350°F (175°C). Grease three 8-inch pans.

2. Mix dry ingredients. In another bowl, mix wet ingredients and combine.

3. Slowly add coffee and mix until batter is smooth.

4. Divide into pans and bake for 25–30 minutes. Cool completely.

5. Whip cream with powdered sugar and vanilla.

6. Layer cake with whipped cream and cherries. Garnish with chocolate and cherries.

German Chocolate Cake

Cake Ingredients:

- 2 cups all-purpose flour
- ¾ cup cocoa powder
- 1 ½ tsp baking soda
- ½ tsp salt
- 1 cup unsalted butter
- 1 ¾ cups sugar
- 4 eggs
- 1 tsp vanilla
- 1 cup buttermilk

Coconut-Pecan Filling:

- 1 cup evaporated milk
- 1 cup sugar
- 3 egg yolks
- ½ cup butter
- 1 tsp vanilla
- 1 ½ cups shredded coconut
- 1 cup chopped pecans

Instructions:

1. Preheat oven to 350°F (175°C). Grease three 8-inch pans.

2. Make the cake: cream butter and sugar, beat in eggs and vanilla, alternate flour mix and buttermilk.

3. Pour into pans and bake 25–30 minutes. Cool.

4. Make the filling: Combine milk, sugar, yolks, butter, and vanilla in a saucepan. Cook on medium until thickened.

5. Stir in coconut and pecans. Cool.

6. Assemble cake with filling between layers. Frost top and sides if desired with more coconut or chocolate ganache.

Peanut Butter Cup Cake

Cake Ingredients:

- 2 cups all-purpose flour
- 1 ½ cups sugar
- ¾ cup cocoa powder
- 1 ½ tsp baking soda
- ½ tsp salt
- ¾ cup vegetable oil
- 1 cup buttermilk
- 2 eggs
- 1 tsp vanilla
- 1 cup hot water or coffee

Peanut Butter Frosting:

- 1 cup peanut butter
- ½ cup butter
- 3 cups powdered sugar
- 3–4 tbsp milk
- 1 tsp vanilla

Ganache Topping:

- ½ cup heavy cream

- ¾ cup chocolate chips

Instructions:

1. Preheat to 350°F (175°C). Line two or three 8-inch pans.

2. Mix wet ingredients, add dry, then stir in hot water. Batter will be thin.

3. Bake 30 minutes or until done. Cool completely.

4. Make frosting: beat peanut butter and butter, add sugar, milk, and vanilla.

5. Ganache: heat cream, pour over chocolate, let sit 1 min, stir smooth.

6. Assemble layers with frosting, drizzle ganache over the top. Decorate with chopped peanut butter cups.

Churro Layer Cake

A delightful cinnamon-sugar cake with layers of spiced goodness, inspired by churros.

Ingredients:

- 2 1/2 cups all-purpose flour
- 2 tsp baking powder
- 1 tsp ground cinnamon
- 1/2 tsp salt
- 1 cup unsalted butter, softened
- 1 1/2 cups granulated sugar
- 3 large eggs
- 1 tsp vanilla extract
- 1 cup whole milk
- 1/4 cup brown sugar (for sprinkling)
- 1 tbsp cinnamon (for sprinkling)

Frosting:

- 1 cup unsalted butter, softened
- 4 cups powdered sugar
- 2 tbsp milk
- 1 tsp vanilla extract

- Pinch of salt

Instructions:

1. Preheat oven to 350°F (175°C). Grease and flour two 9-inch round cake pans.

2. In a bowl, whisk together the flour, baking powder, cinnamon, and salt.

3. In a separate bowl, cream the butter and sugar until light and fluffy. Add the eggs, one at a time, mixing well after each addition, followed by vanilla extract.

4. Alternate adding the dry ingredients and milk, starting and ending with the dry ingredients. Mix until just combined.

5. Divide the batter evenly between the pans and bake for 25-30 minutes, or until a toothpick comes out clean.

6. For the frosting, beat the butter, powdered sugar, milk, vanilla extract, and salt until smooth and fluffy.

7. To assemble, sprinkle the layers of cake with the brown sugar and cinnamon mix before frosting them.

8. Frost the cooled cakes and enjoy the churro-inspired treat!

Hazelnut Praline Cake

A nutty, indulgent cake filled with crunchy praline and rich hazelnut flavor.

Ingredients:

- 2 cups all-purpose flour
- 1 1/2 cups granulated sugar
- 1 tsp baking powder
- 1/2 tsp salt
- 1 cup unsalted butter, softened
- 4 large eggs
- 1 tsp vanilla extract
- 1/2 cup ground hazelnuts
- 1/2 cup whole milk

Praline Filling:

- 1 cup hazelnuts, chopped
- 1/2 cup brown sugar
- 1/2 cup heavy cream
- 1/4 cup unsalted butter

Frosting:

- 1 1/2 cups heavy cream

- 2 tbsp powdered sugar

- 1 tsp vanilla extract

Instructions:

1. Preheat oven to 350°F (175°C). Grease and flour two 9-inch round cake pans.

2. In a bowl, whisk together the flour, sugar, baking powder, and salt.

3. Cream the butter and eggs until light and fluffy. Add the ground hazelnuts and vanilla extract, mixing well.

4. Alternate adding the dry ingredients and milk until combined. Divide the batter between the pans and bake for 25-30 minutes, or until a toothpick comes out clean.

5. For the praline filling, combine the hazelnuts, brown sugar, heavy cream, and butter in a saucepan over medium heat. Stir until the mixture is smooth and thickened.

6. For the frosting, beat the heavy cream, powdered sugar, and vanilla until stiff peaks form.

7. Assemble the cake by layering the praline filling between the cake layers and frosting the entire cake with the whipped cream mixture.

Tiramisu Cake

A moist coffee-flavored cake layered with creamy mascarpone frosting, just like the classic Italian dessert.

Ingredients:

- 2 cups all-purpose flour
- 1 tsp baking powder
- 1/2 tsp salt
- 1 cup unsalted butter, softened
- 1 1/4 cups granulated sugar
- 4 large eggs
- 1 tsp vanilla extract
- 1/2 cup strong brewed coffee (cooled)
- 1/2 cup buttermilk

Frosting:

- 1 1/2 cups mascarpone cheese, softened
- 1 cup heavy cream
- 1/4 cup powdered sugar
- 2 tbsp coffee liqueur (optional)

Instructions:

1. Preheat oven to 350°F (175°C). Grease and flour two 9-inch round cake pans.

2. In a bowl, whisk together the flour, baking powder, and salt.

3. In a separate bowl, cream the butter and sugar until light and fluffy. Add the eggs, one at a time, mixing well after each addition, followed by vanilla extract.

4. Add the coffee and buttermilk alternately with the dry ingredients until just combined. Divide the batter between the pans and bake for 25-30 minutes.

5. For the frosting, whip the mascarpone cheese, heavy cream, powdered sugar, and coffee liqueur (if using) until smooth and fluffy.

6. Assemble the cake by layering the frosting between the cooled cake layers, and top with a dusting of cocoa powder.

Mango Coconut Cake

A tropical, fruity cake with a refreshing mango flavor and a coconut twist.

Ingredients:

- 2 1/2 cups all-purpose flour
- 1 1/2 tsp baking powder
- 1/2 tsp salt
- 1 cup unsalted butter, softened
- 1 1/4 cups granulated sugar
- 3 large eggs
- 1 tsp vanilla extract
- 1/2 cup canned coconut milk
- 1/2 cup fresh mango puree

Frosting:

- 1 cup unsalted butter, softened
- 4 cups powdered sugar
- 1/2 cup coconut milk
- 1/2 cup shredded coconut

Instructions:

1. Preheat oven to 350°F (175°C). Grease and flour two 9-inch round cake pans.

2. In a bowl, whisk together the flour, baking powder, and salt.

3. Cream the butter and sugar until light and fluffy. Add the eggs, one at a time, mixing well after each addition, followed by vanilla extract.

4. Add the coconut milk and mango puree, alternating with the dry ingredients, and mix until smooth. Divide the batter between the pans and bake for 25-30 minutes.

5. For the frosting, beat the butter, powdered sugar, and coconut milk until fluffy. Frost the cooled cakes and sprinkle with shredded coconut.

Pumpkin Spice Layer Cake

A cozy, spiced pumpkin cake perfect for fall celebrations.

Ingredients:

- 2 cups all-purpose flour
- 1 1/2 tsp baking powder
- 1 tsp ground cinnamon
- 1/2 tsp ground nutmeg
- 1/4 tsp ground cloves
- 1/2 tsp salt
- 1 cup unsalted butter, softened
- 1 1/4 cups granulated sugar
- 3 large eggs
- 1 cup canned pumpkin puree
- 1 tsp vanilla extract

Frosting:

- 1 cup unsalted butter, softened
- 4 cups powdered sugar
- 1 tsp vanilla extract
- 2 tbsp heavy cream

Instructions:

1. Preheat oven to 350°F (175°C). Grease and flour two 9-inch round cake pans.

2. In a bowl, whisk together the flour, baking powder, cinnamon, nutmeg, cloves, and salt.

3. Cream the butter and sugar until light and fluffy. Add the eggs one at a time, mixing well after each addition, followed by the pumpkin puree and vanilla extract.

4. Gradually add the dry ingredients to the wet mixture and mix until smooth.

5. Divide the batter between the pans and bake for 25-30 minutes, or until a toothpick comes out clean.

6. For the frosting, beat the butter, powdered sugar, vanilla extract, and heavy cream until smooth. Frost the cooled cakes.

Raspberry Chocolate Cake

A decadent chocolate cake filled with tangy raspberry layers and smooth chocolate frosting.

Ingredients:

- 2 cups all-purpose flour
- 1 1/2 cups granulated sugar
- 1 tsp baking powder
- 1/2 tsp salt
- 1/2 cup unsweetened cocoa powder
- 1 cup unsalted butter, softened
- 3 large eggs
- 1 tsp vanilla extract
- 1 cup buttermilk

Raspberry Filling:

- 2 cups fresh raspberries
- 1/2 cup sugar
- 1 tbsp lemon juice

Frosting:

- 1 1/2 cups heavy cream
- 2 cups semi-sweet chocolate chips

- 1/4 cup powdered sugar

Instructions:

1. Preheat oven to 350°F (175°C). Grease and flour two 9-inch round cake pans.

2. In a bowl, whisk together the flour, sugar, baking powder, salt, and cocoa powder.

3. Cream the butter and eggs until light and fluffy. Add the vanilla extract and alternate adding the dry ingredients and buttermilk. Mix until just combined.

4. For the raspberry filling, cook the raspberries, sugar, and lemon juice over medium heat until thickened.

5. For the frosting, heat the heavy cream in a saucepan until just simmering, then pour over the chocolate chips. Stir until smooth.

6. Assemble the cake by layering raspberry filling and frosting between the cooled cake layers.

Orange Creamsicle Layer Cake

A light, citrusy cake with a smooth, creamy orange filling.

Ingredients:

- 2 1/2 cups all-purpose flour
- 1 1/2 tsp baking powder
- 1/2 tsp salt
- 1 cup unsalted butter, softened
- 1 1/4 cups granulated sugar
- 3 large eggs
- 1 tsp vanilla extract
- 1/2 cup fresh orange juice
- Zest of 1 orange

Frosting:

- 1 cup unsalted butter, softened
- 4 cups powdered sugar
- 1/2 cup fresh orange juice
- 1 tsp vanilla extract

Instructions:

1. Preheat oven to 350°F (175°C). Grease and flour two 9-inch round cake pans.

2. In a bowl, whisk together the flour, baking powder, and salt.

3. Cream the butter and sugar until light and fluffy. Add the eggs one at a time, mixing well after each addition, followed by the vanilla extract, orange juice, and zest.

4. Gradually add the dry ingredients and mix until smooth.

5. Divide the batter between the pans and bake for 25-30 minutes.

6. For the frosting, beat the butter, powdered sugar, orange juice, and vanilla until smooth. Frost the cooled cakes.

Pina Colada Cake

Ingredients

For the Cake:

- 2 ½ cups all-purpose flour
- 2 ½ tsp baking powder
- ½ tsp baking soda
- ½ tsp salt
- 1 cup unsalted butter, softened
- 1 ¾ cups granulated sugar
- 4 eggs
- 1 tsp vanilla extract
- ½ tsp coconut extract (optional)
- ½ cup crushed pineapple (drained)
- ¾ cup canned coconut milk (or whole milk)
- ½ cup sour cream

For the Pineapple Filling (optional but amazing):

- 1 cup crushed pineapple
- ¼ cup sugar
- 1 tbsp cornstarch

- 1 tbsp lemon juice

For the Coconut Cream Frosting:

- 1 cup unsalted butter, softened
- 4 oz cream cheese, softened
- 4 cups powdered sugar
- 2 tbsp coconut milk (or regular milk)
- 1 tsp vanilla or coconut extract

To Garnish:

- Sweetened shredded coconut (toasted or plain)
- Pineapple slices or chunks
- Maraschino cherries (optional)

Instructions

1. Make the Cake:

- Preheat oven to 350°F (175°C). Grease and flour two 9-inch cake pans.
- In a medium bowl, whisk flour, baking powder, baking soda, and salt.
- In a large bowl, cream butter and sugar until light and fluffy. Add eggs one at a time, then mix in vanilla and coconut extract.
- Add sour cream, pineapple, and coconut milk. Mix until well combined.
- Gradually add the dry ingredients, mixing just until smooth.

- Divide the batter between the prepared pans and bake for 30–35 minutes.
- Cool in pans for 10 minutes, then remove and cool completely on a wire rack.

2. Pineapple Filling (Optional):

- Combine crushed pineapple, sugar, cornstarch, and lemon juice in a small pot.
- Simmer over medium heat until thickened (about 5–7 minutes). Let cool.

3. Make the Frosting:

- Beat butter and cream cheese until creamy.
- Add powdered sugar gradually, then mix in vanilla and coconut milk until smooth and fluffy.

4. Assemble the Cake:

- If using pineapple filling, spread it between the cake layers.
- Frost the top and sides with coconut cream frosting.
- Press shredded coconut onto the sides and top.
- Garnish with pineapple and cherries if desired.

Key Lime Cake

A tart and sweet citrus cake with zesty lime flavor.

Ingredients:

- 2 1/2 cups all-purpose flour
- 1 1/2 tsp baking powder
- 1/4 tsp salt
- 1 cup unsalted butter, softened
- 1 1/4 cups granulated sugar
- 3 large eggs
- 1/2 cup key lime juice
- Zest of 2 key limes

Frosting:

- 1 cup cream cheese
- 1/2 cup butter
- 4 cups powdered sugar
- 1 tbsp key lime juice

Instructions:

1. Preheat oven to 350°F (175°C). Grease and flour cake pans.
2. Mix dry ingredients in a bowl.

3. In another bowl, cream butter and sugar, add eggs, key lime juice, and zest.

4. Combine wet and dry ingredients. Bake 25–30 minutes.

5. Frost with cream cheese, butter, powdered sugar, and lime juice.

Bourbon Pecan Cake

Ingredients

Cake:

- 2 cups all-purpose flour
- 2 tsp baking powder
- ½ tsp baking soda
- ½ tsp salt
- 1 tsp cinnamon
- ½ tsp nutmeg
- 1 cup unsalted butter, softened
- 1½ cups brown sugar
- 4 large eggs
- ⅓ cup bourbon
- ¾ cup sour cream
- 1 tsp vanilla extract
- 1 cup toasted pecans, chopped

Glaze:

- ¼ cup butter
- ½ cup brown sugar

- 2 tbsp heavy cream
- 2 tbsp bourbon

Instructions

1. Preheat oven to 350°F. Grease and flour a bundt or round cake pan.
2. Mix flour, baking powder, baking soda, salt, cinnamon, and nutmeg.
3. Cream butter and brown sugar. Add eggs one at a time.
4. Stir in bourbon, sour cream, and vanilla. Add dry ingredients gradually.
5. Fold in pecans and pour into pan.
6. Bake 35–40 mins. Cool before glazing.
7. For glaze: melt butter, add sugar and cream, simmer, stir in bourbon. Drizzle over cake.

Cherry Almond Cake

Ingredients

Cake:

- 1½ cups all-purpose flour
- 1 tsp baking powder
- ¼ tsp salt
- ½ cup unsalted butter, softened
- ¾ cup granulated sugar
- 2 large eggs
- ½ tsp almond extract
- ½ cup milk
- 1 cup chopped fresh or maraschino cherries
- ⅓ cup sliced almonds

Frosting:

- ½ cup butter, softened
- 2 cups powdered sugar
- 1–2 tbsp cherry juice
- ¼ tsp almond extract

Instructions

1. Preheat oven to 350°F. Line or grease an 8-inch round pan.

2. Whisk flour, baking powder, and salt.

3. Cream butter and sugar. Beat in eggs, almond extract, and milk.

4. Fold in cherries and almonds. Pour into pan.

5. Bake for 30–35 mins. Cool completely.

6. Make frosting: beat butter, sugar, juice, and extract until smooth. Frost cooled cake.

Snickers Layer Cake

Ingredients

Cake:

- 2 cups all-purpose flour
- ¾ cup unsweetened cocoa powder
- 1½ tsp baking soda
- 1 tsp baking powder
- ½ tsp salt
- 1 cup granulated sugar
- 1 cup brown sugar
- 2 large eggs
- ½ cup vegetable oil
- 1 cup buttermilk
- 1 tsp vanilla extract
- 1 cup hot coffee

Filling:

- 1 cup caramel sauce
- 1½ cups chopped Snickers bars

Frosting:

- 1 cup butter

- ½ cup cocoa powder

- 3 cups powdered sugar

- ¼ cup milk

- 1 tsp vanilla extract

Instructions

1. Preheat oven to 350°F. Prepare 2–3 round cake pans.

2. Combine dry ingredients. In a separate bowl, whisk sugars, eggs, oil, buttermilk, and vanilla.

3. Add dry ingredients, then stir in hot coffee.

4. Divide batter into pans. Bake 30–35 mins.

5. Cool and layer with caramel and chopped Snickers.

6. Make frosting: beat butter, cocoa, sugar, milk, and vanilla until fluffy. Frost and garnish with extra Snickers.

White Chocolate Strawberry Cake

Ingredients

Cake:

- 2¼ cups cake flour
- 1 tbsp baking powder
- ½ tsp salt
- ¾ cup unsalted butter
- 1½ cups sugar
- 4 egg whites
- 1 tsp vanilla extract
- ⅓ cup sour cream
- ½ cup milk
- ⅔ cup chopped fresh strawberries
- 4 oz white chocolate, melted

Frosting:

- 1 cup unsalted butter
- 3 cups powdered sugar
- ½ cup melted white chocolate
- 1 tsp vanilla extract

- 2–3 tbsp cream or milk

Instructions

1. Preheat oven to 350°F. Prepare cake pans.

2. Mix dry ingredients. Cream butter and sugar. Add egg whites, vanilla, and sour cream.

3. Add flour and milk gradually. Fold in strawberries and white chocolate.

4. Bake 25–30 mins. Cool completely.

5. For frosting: beat butter, sugar, white chocolate, vanilla, and cream. Frost the cake.

Cookies and Cream Cake

Ingredients

Cake:

- 1¾ cups all-purpose flour
- ½ cup cocoa powder
- 1½ tsp baking powder
- 1 tsp baking soda
- ½ tsp salt
- ¾ cup unsalted butter
- 1½ cups sugar
- 2 large eggs
- 1 tsp vanilla extract
- 1 cup buttermilk
- 10 crushed Oreo cookies

Frosting:

- 1 cup butter
- 2½ cups powdered sugar
- 2 tbsp milk
- ½ tsp vanilla extract

- 8 crushed Oreos

Instructions

1. Preheat oven to 350°F. Prepare pans.

2. Combine dry ingredients. Cream butter and sugar. Add eggs and vanilla.

3. Alternate flour and buttermilk into the mix. Stir in crushed Oreos.

4. Bake 30–35 mins. Cool completely.

5. For frosting: beat butter, sugar, milk, vanilla, and Oreos. Frost the cake and decorate with extra cookies.

Zucchini Chocolate Cake

Ingredients

Cake:

- 2 cups grated zucchini
- 1¾ cups all-purpose flour
- ½ cup cocoa powder
- 1½ tsp baking soda
- ½ tsp salt
- 1 cup sugar
- ½ cup brown sugar
- ¾ cup vegetable oil
- 2 large eggs
- 1 tsp vanilla extract
- ½ cup sour cream
- ½ cup chocolate chips

Frosting (optional):

- ½ cup butter
- ½ cup cocoa powder
- 2½ cups powdered sugar

- ¼ cup milk
- 1 tsp vanilla

Instructions

1. Preheat oven to 350°F. Grease a 9x13-inch pan.
2. Mix dry ingredients. In another bowl, combine sugars, oil, eggs, vanilla, and sour cream.
3. Stir in zucchini. Add dry ingredients, mix well.
4. Fold in chocolate chips. Pour into pan and bake for 35–40 mins.
5. Cool. Make frosting: beat all ingredients until fluffy. Frost if desired.

Coconut Pineapple Cake

Ingredients

Cake:

- 1½ cups all-purpose flour
- 1 tsp baking powder
- ½ tsp baking soda
- ¼ tsp salt
- 1 cup granulated sugar
- ½ cup unsalted butter, softened
- 2 large eggs
- 1 tsp vanilla extract
- ¾ cup canned pineapple (drained and crushed)
- ¼ cup coconut flakes
- ½ cup milk

Frosting:

- 1 cup unsalted butter, softened
- 4 cups powdered sugar
- ¼ cup coconut milk

- 1 tsp vanilla extract

- ½ cup coconut flakes

Instructions

1. Preheat oven to 350°F. Grease and flour a round cake pan.

2. Whisk flour, baking powder, baking soda, and salt.

3. Beat sugar and butter until fluffy. Add eggs and vanilla, mix.

4. Stir in pineapple, coconut, and milk, then fold in dry ingredients.

5. Pour batter into pan. Bake for 25–30 mins.

6. For frosting: Beat butter, powdered sugar, coconut milk, and vanilla until smooth. Frost cooled cake. Garnish with coconut flakes.

Maple Walnut Cake

Ingredients

Cake:

- 2 cups all-purpose flour
- 2 tsp baking powder
- ½ tsp salt
- 1 tsp cinnamon
- ½ cup unsalted butter, softened
- 1 cup brown sugar
- 2 large eggs
- ½ cup maple syrup
- 1 cup milk
- 1 cup walnuts, chopped

Frosting:

- 1 cup unsalted butter, softened
- 2 cups powdered sugar
- ¼ cup maple syrup
- 1 tsp vanilla extract

Instructions

1. Preheat oven to 350°F. Grease a round cake pan.

2. Whisk dry ingredients.

3. Cream butter and sugar. Add eggs and maple syrup, mixing well.

4. Alternate adding dry ingredients and milk. Fold in walnuts.

5. Bake for 30–35 mins. Cool completely.

6. For frosting: Beat butter, powdered sugar, maple syrup, and vanilla until fluffy. Frost the cake.

Mocha Hazelnut Cake

Ingredients

Cake:

- 1¾ cups all-purpose flour
- ½ cup cocoa powder
- 1 tsp baking soda
- ½ tsp salt
- 1 tsp instant coffee powder
- 1 cup granulated sugar
- ½ cup unsalted butter, softened
- 2 large eggs
- 1 tsp vanilla extract
- 1 cup milk
- ½ cup ground hazelnuts

Frosting:

- 1 cup unsalted butter, softened
- 2½ cups powdered sugar
- ¼ cup cocoa powder

- 2 tbsp instant coffee

- 2 tbsp milk

- ½ cup chopped hazelnuts (for garnish)

Instructions

1. Preheat oven to 350°F. Grease two round cake pans.

2. Whisk flour, cocoa, baking soda, salt, and coffee powder.

3. Beat sugar and butter until fluffy. Add eggs and vanilla, mix well.

4. Add dry ingredients alternately with milk. Stir in ground hazelnuts.

5. Pour into pans and bake for 30–35 mins. Cool completely.

6. For frosting: Beat butter, powdered sugar, cocoa, coffee, and milk until smooth. Frost the cake and garnish with hazelnuts.

S'mores Layer Cake

Ingredients

Cake:

- 2 cups all-purpose flour
- 1 cup cocoa powder
- 1½ tsp baking powder
- 1 tsp baking soda
- ½ tsp salt
- 1 cup granulated sugar
- ½ cup brown sugar
- 1 cup buttermilk
- 2 large eggs
- 1 tsp vanilla extract
- 1 cup mini marshmallows

Filling:

- 1 cup chocolate ganache
- 1 cup crushed graham crackers

Frosting:

- 1 cup unsalted butter, softened
- 2 cups powdered sugar
- 3 tbsp cocoa powder
- 2 tbsp milk
- 1 tsp vanilla extract
- 1 cup mini marshmallows

Instructions

1. Preheat oven to 350°F. Grease and flour round cake pans.
2. Whisk dry ingredients. Beat sugar, butter, and eggs until fluffy.
3. Add buttermilk and vanilla. Gradually add dry ingredients. Stir in marshmallows.
4. Pour batter into pans and bake for 30–35 mins. Cool completely.
5. For filling: Spread ganache and crushed graham crackers between layers.
6. For frosting: Beat butter, powdered sugar, cocoa, milk, and vanilla until smooth. Frost cake and top with marshmallows.

Lavender Honey Cake

Ingredients

Cake:

- 2 cups all-purpose flour
- 1 tsp baking powder
- ½ tsp baking soda
- ¼ tsp salt
- 2 tsp dried lavender flowers
- 1 cup granulated sugar
- ½ cup unsalted butter, softened
- 2 large eggs
- ½ cup honey
- 1 tsp vanilla extract
- 1 cup buttermilk

Frosting:

- 1 cup unsalted butter, softened
- 3 cups powdered sugar
- 2 tbsp honey

- 1 tsp vanilla extract

- 1 tsp dried lavender flowers (optional)

Instructions

1. Preheat oven to 350°F. Grease and flour cake pans.

2. Whisk flour, baking powder, baking soda, salt, and lavender.

3. Cream butter and sugar. Add eggs, honey, and vanilla, mixing well.

4. Add dry ingredients alternately with buttermilk.

5. Bake for 25–30 mins. Cool completely.

6. For frosting: Beat butter, powdered sugar, honey, and vanilla. Frost the cake. Garnish with lavender if desired.

Chocolate Mint Layer Cake

Ingredients

Cake:

- 2 cups all-purpose flour
- 1½ cups cocoa powder
- 1½ tsp baking powder
- 1 tsp baking soda
- ½ tsp salt
- 1 cup granulated sugar
- 1 cup brown sugar
- 2 large eggs
- 1 tsp peppermint extract
- 1 cup buttermilk
- ½ cup vegetable oil

Frosting:

- 1 cup unsalted butter, softened
- 3 cups powdered sugar
- 2 tbsp cocoa powder

- 1 tsp peppermint extract

- 3 tbsp milk

Instructions

1. Preheat oven to 350°F. Grease and flour cake pans.

2. Whisk dry ingredients. Beat sugar, butter, eggs, and peppermint until fluffy.

3. Add buttermilk and oil. Gradually fold in dry ingredients.

4. Bake for 30–35 mins. Cool completely.

5. For frosting: Beat butter, powdered sugar, cocoa, peppermint extract, and milk. Frost the cake.

Lemon Poppy Seed Cake

Ingredients:

- 2 1/4 cups all-purpose flour
- 1 tbsp poppy seeds
- 1 tsp baking powder
- 1/2 tsp baking soda
- 1/4 tsp salt
- 1 cup butter
- 1 cup sugar
- 4 eggs
- 1/2 cup sour cream
- Juice & zest of 2 lemons
- 1 tsp vanilla

Glaze:

- 1 cup powdered sugar
- 2–3 tbsp lemon juice

Instructions:

1. Preheat oven to 350°F (175°C). Grease and flour two 9-inch pans.
2. Cream butter and sugar. Add eggs, sour cream, lemon juice, zest, and vanilla.

3. Mix dry ingredients. Stir into wet until just combined.

4. Divide into pans. Bake 30–35 minutes. Cool. Drizzle with glaze.

Red Wine Chocolate Cake

Ingredients:

- 1 3/4 cups all-purpose flour
- 3/4 cup unsweetened cocoa powder
- 1 tsp baking powder
- 1/2 tsp salt
- 1/2 cup butter
- 1/4 cup oil
- 1 1/2 cups sugar
- 2 eggs + 1 yolk
- 1 tsp vanilla
- 1 cup dry red wine

Frosting:

- 1 cup dark chocolate chips
- 1/2 cup heavy cream
- 1 tbsp butter

Instructions:

1. Preheat oven to 350°F (175°C). Grease two 9-inch pans.
2. Cream butter, oil, and sugar. Beat in eggs and vanilla.

3. Mix dry ingredients separately. Alternately add dry mix and wine to the wet mix.

4. Bake for 30–35 minutes. Cool. Frost with ganache (melt chocolate and butter in cream).

Chai Spice Layer Cake

Ingredients:

- 2 1/2 cups flour
- 1 tbsp chai spice blend (or mix cinnamon, ginger, cardamom, cloves, nutmeg)
- 1/2 tsp salt
- 1 tbsp baking powder
- 1 cup brown sugar
- 1 cup butter
- 4 eggs
- 1 tsp vanilla
- 1 cup milk (steeped with 2 chai tea bags and cooled)

Frosting:

- 1/2 cup butter
- 8 oz cream cheese
- 1 tsp cinnamon
- 3 cups powdered sugar

Instructions:

1. Preheat oven to 350°F (175°C). Grease and line three 8-inch pans.
2. Cream butter and sugar. Add eggs, vanilla, and chai-steeped milk.

3. Combine dry ingredients. Add to wet mix.

4. Bake 25–30 minutes. Cool. Frost with spiced cream cheese frosting.

Lemon Raspberry Cheesecake Cake

Ingredients:

Lemon Cake:

- 2 1/2 cups flour
- 2 tsp baking powder
- 1/2 tsp salt
- 1 cup butter
- 1 1/4 cups sugar
- 4 eggs
- Zest of 2 lemons
- 1/2 cup lemon juice
- 1/2 cup sour cream

Raspberry Cheesecake Layer:

- 16 oz cream cheese
- 1/2 cup sugar
- 2 eggs
- 1/2 cup sour cream
- 1/2 cup raspberry puree or swirl

Frosting:

- 8 oz cream cheese

- 1/2 cup butter

- 4 cups powdered sugar

- 1 tbsp lemon juice

Instructions:

1. Bake cheesecake layer first: Mix ingredients, swirl in raspberry, and bake in a springform pan at 325°F (160°C) for 40–45 minutes. Cool completely.

2. Bake lemon cake: Cream butter and sugar, add eggs, zest, juice, sour cream. Mix dry ingredients and combine. Bake in two 9-inch pans for 25–30 minutes.

3. Stack lemon cake, cheesecake, then lemon cake. Frost and decorate with raspberries.

Coffee Hazelnut Cake

Ingredients:

- 2 cups all-purpose flour
- 1 tbsp instant espresso powder
- 1 tsp baking powder
- 1/2 tsp baking soda
- 1/2 tsp salt
- 1/2 cup ground hazelnuts (toasted)
- 1 cup butter
- 1 cup brown sugar
- 3 eggs
- 1/2 cup sour cream
- 1/2 cup strong brewed coffee
- 1 tsp vanilla extract

Frosting:

- 1/2 cup butter
- 1/4 cup espresso or coffee
- 3 cups powdered sugar
- 1/2 cup finely chopped hazelnuts (for garnish)

Instructions:

1. Preheat oven to 350°F (175°C). Prepare two 8-inch pans.

2. Cream butter and sugar. Add eggs one by one, then vanilla.

3. Mix dry ingredients. Alternate adding dry mix and sour cream/coffee.

4. Divide and bake for 30–35 mins. Cool and frost. Sprinkle chopped hazelnuts on top.

Nutella Hazelnut Cake

Ingredients:

- 1 1/2 cups flour
- 1 tsp baking powder
- 1/2 tsp salt
- 1/2 cup butter
- 3/4 cup sugar
- 3 eggs
- 1/2 cup milk
- 1 tsp vanilla
- 1/2 cup Nutella
- 1/2 cup ground hazelnuts

Frosting:

- 1 cup Nutella
- 1/2 cup butter
- 3 cups powdered sugar
- 2 tbsp milk (as needed)

Instructions:

1. Preheat oven to 350°F (175°C). Grease two 8-inch pans.

2. Cream butter and sugar. Add eggs and vanilla.

3. Mix dry ingredients. Add milk and Nutella alternately with dry mix.

4. Pour and bake 30–35 mins. Cool. Frost with Nutella frosting.

Choco-Mocha Torte

Ingredients:

- 1 1/4 cups flour
- 1/2 cup cocoa powder
- 1/2 tsp baking soda
- 1/2 tsp salt
- 3/4 cup butter
- 1 cup sugar
- 2 eggs
- 1 tsp vanilla
- 1/2 cup strong brewed coffee
- 1/2 cup sour cream

Frosting:

- 1 cup dark chocolate, melted
- 1/2 cup heavy cream
- 1 tsp instant coffee powder

Instructions:

1. Preheat to 350°F (175°C). Prepare two 8-inch pans.

2. Mix dry ingredients. Cream butter and sugar, then add eggs, vanilla, coffee, and sour cream.

3. Combine wet and dry. Pour and bake 30 minutes.

4. Cool and frost with mocha ganache.

Mixed Berry Yogurt Cake

Ingredients:

- 2 cups all-purpose flour
- 2 tsp baking powder
- 1/4 tsp salt
- 1/2 cup butter
- 1 cup sugar
- 3 eggs
- 1 cup plain Greek yogurt
- 1 tsp vanilla
- 1 1/2 cups mixed berries (fresh or frozen)

Topping:

- Whipped cream
- Extra berries for garnish

Instructions:

1. Preheat oven to 350°F (175°C). Line two pans.
2. Cream butter and sugar. Add eggs, yogurt, and vanilla.
3. Fold in dry ingredients and gently stir in berries.
4. Bake for 30–35 mins. Cool and top with whipped cream and berries.

Sweet Potato Spice Cake

Ingredients:

- 2 cups mashed sweet potatoes
- 2 cups all-purpose flour
- 2 tsp cinnamon
- 1/2 tsp nutmeg
- 1/4 tsp cloves
- 1/2 tsp salt
- 2 tsp baking powder
- 1 cup brown sugar
- 3/4 cup vegetable oil
- 4 eggs

Frosting:

- 1/2 cup butter
- 8 oz cream cheese
- 1 tsp vanilla
- 3 cups powdered sugar

Instructions:

1. Preheat oven to 350°F (175°C). Prepare two 9-inch pans.

2. Mix all dry ingredients in a bowl. In another bowl, mix sweet potato, oil, sugar, and eggs.

3. Combine and pour into pans. Bake 35 mins. Frost when cool.

Oreo Cookie Layer Cake

Ingredients:

- 2 cups flour
- 3/4 cup cocoa powder
- 1 1/2 tsp baking powder
- 1/2 tsp salt
- 1 cup sugar
- 1 cup brown sugar
- 3 eggs
- 1/2 cup oil
- 1 cup milk
- 1 tsp vanilla
- 12 crushed Oreos

Frosting:

- 1/2 cup butter
- 1/2 cup shortening
- 3 cups powdered sugar
- 1 tsp vanilla
- 1/4 cup crushed Oreos

Instructions:

1. Preheat to 350°F (175°C). Grease and line two 8-inch pans.

2. Mix dry ingredients. Cream eggs, sugar, oil, vanilla, and milk.

3. Fold in crushed Oreos. Bake 30–35 mins. Cool and frost.

Cinnamon Roll Layer Cake

Ingredients:

- 2 1/2 cups all-purpose flour
- 2 tsp baking powder
- 1/2 tsp baking soda
- 1 tsp cinnamon
- 1/4 tsp nutmeg
- 1/2 tsp salt
- 3/4 cup butter
- 1 1/2 cups sugar
- 4 eggs
- 1 cup buttermilk
- 2 tsp vanilla

Cinnamon Swirl:

- 1/2 cup brown sugar
- 2 tbsp cinnamon
- 3 tbsp melted butter

Cream Cheese Frosting:

- 8 oz cream cheese

- 1/2 cup butter

- 1 tsp vanilla

- 3-4 cups powdered sugar

Instructions:

1. Preheat to 350°F (175°C). Line and grease three 8-inch pans.

2. Make cake batter. Layer in pans with cinnamon swirl in between.

3. Bake 30-35 minutes. Cool. Frost with cream cheese frosting.

www.ingramcontent.com/pod-product-compliance
Lightning Source LLC
LaVergne TN
LVHW061939070526
838199LV00060B/3881